Buttons and Trimmings

Buttons and Trimmings

by Althea Mackenzie

Special Photography by Richard Blakey

THE NATIONAL TRUST

Introduction

The Wade Collection is not only one of the major collections of costume owned by the National Trust, but also represents a private collection of world-class quality.

Its creator, Charles Paget Wade, was born in 1883. His father was part-owner of a family sugar plantation in St Kitts so that he was brought up in comfortable circumstances, although his childhood with his grandmother in Great Yarmouth in Norfolk was spartan. An instinct for collecting was acquired early, along with a strong sense of place and heritage.

However, the world around him was rapidly changing, compounded by the social, political and economic impact of the First World War. For Wade, this meant that much of what he had relied on as a valuable reference was being destroyed by a society that looked away from the past, and forward to a notion of progress based on material wealth and mass production. Traditional modes and mores were seen as unsustainable and undesirable.

Wade's response was to begin collecting objects that reflected man's craftsmanship and ingenuity. This was very much in tune with the ideals and beliefs of exponents of the Arts & Crafts Movement, such as the architects M.H. Baillie Scott and Sir Edwin Lutyens. In 1919 he bought Snowshill, a derelict but largely unspoilt Cotswold manor, and set about restoring the house and garden drawing on the fundamental principles of Arts & Crafts.

The manor house at Snowshill was the repository for his collections, which covered an astonishing range, from scientific instruments to samurai armour, from cabinets to clocks, from bicycles to kitchen bygones. Wade himself lived in the next door priest's house, to give over maximum space to the objects. In 1948 he decided to hand over his house, gardens and collections to the National Trust. James Lees-Milne, who was responsible for negotiating the transfer of historic houses to the care of the Trust, found Wade the most eccentric of all the owners he had to deal with – no mean feat in a contest replete with eccentric contenders.

In his diary, Lees-Milne drew a vivid pen portrait of Wade: 'Wearing square-cut, shoulder-length, Roundhead hair and dressed in trunk and hose, this magpie collector would, while showing visitors over the house, suddenly disappear behind a tapestry panel to emerge through a secret door on a different level.'

Wade was, in fact, wearing some examples from his magnificent costume collection. This consists of over 2,200 items, the majority dating from the 18th and 19th centuries, many unique and most of astounding quality. Geographically the collection incorporates

material from diverse cultures; for example, from Africa, Russia and the Middle East. Historically it provides a comprehensive record of changing fashions before the impact of uniformity brought about by the effects of industrial revolution and mass production. The range is vast: 18th- and 19th-century dresses (many unaltered), complete men's suits from the 18th century, beautifully embroidered 18th- and 19th-century men's waistcoats, military uniforms, servants' clothes, ecclesiastical costume, accessories such as hats and shoes. The collection is unusual in that Wade valued the utilitarian and mundane as well as the rare and precious.

Originally Wade kept the costume collection in cupboards, drawers and on display in Occidens, a room so named to evoke associations of the West and the setting sun. The clothes also provided an authentic wardrobe for some of the amateur dramatics that were performed at Snowshill, with friends such as John Betjeman, J.B. Priestley, Lutyens and Virginia Woolf. He intended that a special gallery should be built, but the plan was abandoned with the outbreak of the Second World War. On behalf of the National Trust, the collection was looked after and catalogued by the costume historian Nancy Bradfield, and subsequently by the Trust's own conservators at their studio at Blickling Hall in Norfolk.

Now, while all the other collections remain at Snowshill, the costumes and accessories are housed at Berrington Hall in Herefordshire. Because of the constraints of space, it is primarily a reserve collection available for viewing by appointment. The vulnerability innate in costume restricts display opportunities, although portions of the collection are regularly on display at Snowshill and at Berrington. However, access is vital, and this volume, the fourth of a series illustrated with specially commissioned photographs, is one way of enabling readers world-wide to enjoy such an important collection.

We have used the rich resource of the Wade costume collection to show a variety of buttons and trimmings. The first part of the book focuses on buttons from men's dress of the late 18th and early 19th centuries. Although buttons have always performed a practical function, they have also provided a medium for decoration and elaboration, and during the Georgian period men delighted in displaying their status and wealth in the most flamboyant way.

Bone, horn and wood were the traditional bases or formers for buttons, but in the 18th century decorative covers would often be applied. It became fashionable to use a whole range of metals and

alloys such as gold, silver gilt, plate, pewter, steel and brass. Cloth-covered buttons were generally made from brocade, velvet, or the cloth of the garment onto which they were to be attached. By the end of the 18th century, Birmingham had become the centre of button-making, along with a whole variety of small metal objects such as seals, tweezers, corkscrews, and buckles. Men involved in this industry were known as 'toymakers'.

The second part of the book concentrates on trimmings in a whole range of materials, from laces and braids to ribbons, sequins and tassels. Like buttons, they provide opportunities for elaboration and, at times, ostentatious display, memorably summed up by Mrs Hannah Cowley in her comedy *Who's a Dupe?* in 1779: 'What with satins, tassels, and spangles and foils, you look as fine as a chemist's shop by candlelight'.

In 18th– and 19th–century Britain, however wealthy an individual might be, he or she still remodelled and reformed costume and accessories, and here ribbons and trims played an important part. While the Purefoys of Shalstone in Buckinghamshire bought most of their clothes from London in the mid-18th century, they also called upon local suppliers for specific items. Another source for trimmings was the travelling salesmen, markets and fairs, who dominated rural areas until the 19th century, when increasing disposable wealth led to the establishment of a greater number of specialist shops.

The invention of the sewing machine in 1845 meant that trimmings were much cheaper to buy and could be produced in much larger quantities. It is at this stage that Wade's collection becomes sparse: he was primarily interested in hand craftmanship, preferring to concentrate on periods more directly in touch with the methods of production and design.

I would like to thank Richard Blakey for his patience and skill in taking the photographs, Stuart Smith for his designer's artistic eye, Margaret Willes, my publisher, and her assistant Andrew Cummins for coordinating all the disparate elements, of which there have been many.

Lastly, I am grateful to the staff at Berrington Hall and Snowshill Manor for their support.

Althea Mackenzie
Curator of the Wade Costume Collection

Pompeo Batoni's portrait of George Lucy painted in 1758. Lucy wears a court coat of blue velvet with gold embroidered front edges, deep cuffs and pocket flaps, over a white satin waistcoat embroidered with sprigs of flowers and gold wire laid in a scrolling pattern. The buttons of both garments are covered in gold cloth.

Many of the finest examples of decorative buttons in Wade's collection are to be found on men's 18th-century court costume, and in particular coats. These were worn by gentlemen at social occasions, but above all for attendance at the royal court. The court by its very nature encouraged a competitive spirit in terms of design and expenditure. Many contemporary writings refer to the extravagance of such occasions as the marriage in 1734 of the Princess Royal, eldest daughter of George II, to William, Prince of Orange. Mrs Delany recorded: 'The King was in a gold stuff which made much more show, with diamond buttons on his coat'.

This detail comes from a court coat dating from the 1780s, made from fancy silk velvet with a pattern of voided stripes and squares in black, pink and green. It is richly embroidered with metal thread, sequins, silk thread and paste jewels in a flowing design of flowers and leaves (see also pp.70-1). The coat is fastened with 2 metal hooks and eyes, and the buttons are thus purely decorative, 10 running down the centre front, 3 on the cuffs and 3 beneath each of the pocket flaps. The buttons are richly decorated with metal thread, sequins and paste jewels over a wooden or bone former.

Cloth-covered buttons were often embroidered prior to attachment to the bone or wooden former. The design would be marked out at the same time as the embroidery on the unmade coat, before being made up for the individual client. The buttons shown here would have had their flower decoration embroidered in such a manner.

These details are from a man's court coat dating from the 1780s of a very fine burgundy napped wool, the colour and fabric indicating winter wear. The dark wool background provides a perfect foil for the lavish embroidery on the cuffs, the front, the back pleats and collar.

The design is a wonderful composition of flowers and grasses in vivid multi-coloured threads with additional decorative elements that include cascades of sequins, metal thread embroidery, spangles and silk gauze. The total creates a flow and movement with a three-dimensionality that would have been enhanced in the flickering candlelight.

Detail from the waistcoat of
a complete man's suit dating
from the 1770s. The suit,
comprising coat, waistcoat and
knee breeches, is made from
a burgundy silk voided velvet
producing a complex striped
pattern (left). All three com-
ponents are decorated with an
embroidered design of flowers
and leaves interspersed with
paste 'jewels' and sequins
to catch the light and draw
attention to the decoration
(see pp. 12-3 and 72-3).

The buttons are large and
flat, and embroidered to
complement the whole design.
Attempts were made in the
early part of the 18th century,
when cloth-covered buttons
were much in fashion, to
protect the livelihood of the
metal button producers based
in the English Midlands, and in
particular in Birmingham. Acts
were passed during the reigns
of Queen Anne and George I
to make illegal the wearing of
cloth-covered buttons. This
proved impossible to enforce,
but Birmingham and other
Midlands towns compensated
for this loss by becoming the
centres for producing the metal
shanks that attached buttons to
garments.

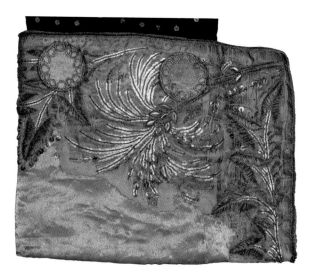

Details of a late 18th-century coat made from a deep beetroot silk velvet decorated with all-over sequins of silver (see also pp.74-5). The front, the back pleats and the pocket flaps are all decorated with a design of palm trees and other exotic foliage executed in sequins and metal thread embroidery. The cuffs (one of which is shown above) are of cream silk ribbed with fine silver thread to give the appearance of cloth of silver. The coat is further decorated with large flat buttons covered with silver foil, silver threads and paste jewels.

Paste is glass with a high lead content that has the effect of creating a glistening, gem-like quality. As a result it has often been used as a substitute for gemstones, notably by the Romans and the Anglo-Saxons, and during the Italian Renaissance. It was during the 18th century that the use of paste jewels came into its own in Britain – so much so that at one point they became subject to tax.

This coat is possibly of Indian manufacture. It was common practice for traders and colonists to take advantage of sumptuous materials and cheap labour to have such exotic garments made.

Waistcoat

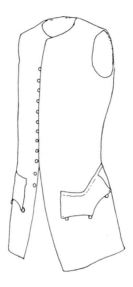

Sir Rowland Winn, a portrait painted by Henry Pickering in 1746, now at Nostell Priory in Yorkshire. Winn is wearing basket buttons on his waistcoat of gold satin decorated with silver lace around the edges and on the pocket flaps.

The buttons on this waistcoat dating from the 1760s are known as basket buttons. This type of button was also known as Leek, from the Staffordshire town where the speciality was producing silk thread worked in a basket weave pattern on a button mould. Here silver thread passes over the former and silver foil in a lattice design.

The shape is slightly domed, the characteristic style up to the 1780s when flatter buttons came into fashion.

The basket buttons shown here complement the silver design on the waistcoat which is brocaded onto beryl blue silk satin. The design, which decorates the front and the pocket flaps, is of bunches of snowdrops joined together with stylised leaves which increase in size and include daffodils at the lower edge.

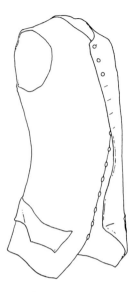

Detail from a waistcoat dating from 1775-85. By this period the decoration on waistcoats was less strictly focused on the edges and pocket flaps, but tended to include an all-over patterning. This example is typical of the movement towards lighter fabrics and embroidery. The delicate silk taffeta is decorated with exquisite metal threadwork in a design of silver leaves and gold flowers on the leading edges and pocket flaps. The buttons are beautifully composed of metal thread in the quartered pattern known as death's head.

Detail from a double-breasted waistcoat dating from the 1780s. By this period costume was beginning to be influenced by the ideological changes associated with the French Revolution and the adoption of classical principles. Gone were the exotic embroidered court coats shown on previous pages. Instead, men wore plain dark woollen coats, with their waistcoats generally moving towards a sharper line with square-cut base, welted pockets, small lapels and stand collars. *The Gentleman's and London Magazine* of 1777 observed, 'The waistcoat worn a few years ago would now make two; the length is now so shallow.'

This style of exquisite tailoring that revealed the male figure was devised by Beau Brummell and his circle, and adopted by the 'dandies'.

The example shown here is made from striped silk satin. The buttons are also decorated with a geometric pattern made up of crossing threads in four colours, the style known as death's head. There are 18 buttons closing the waistcoat. This particular style of waistcoat became known as the 'Newmarket'.

Detail from a group portrait of the Lukin brothers, painted by William Redmore Bigg in 1802 and now at Felbrigg Hall in Norfolk. Two of the brothers, shown here with their gamekeeper, have the fashionable short waistcoats of the period, the one on the left is striped, that on the right plain.

Detail from a waistcoat with death's head buttons made in the 1780s. This double-breasted waistcoat is similar to the previous example. It is made from a silk brocade with a geometric chequered design consisting of a colour combination of moss green, parchment, black, vanilla and beryl blue. It fastens with 26 death's head buttons that echo the colours of the brocade, but contrast in pattern to bring the whole design to life.

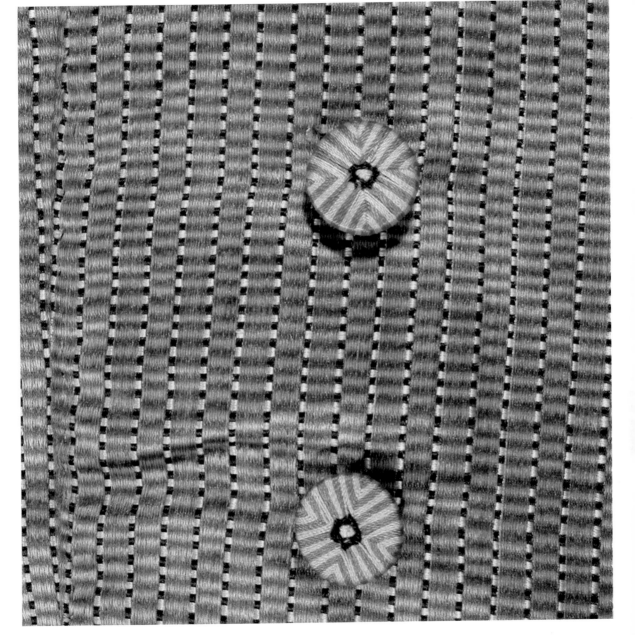

Like the detail of the waistcoats shown on pp. 18-21, this is a fine example of a late 18th-century waistcoat made from a geometric patterned silk. Here the pattern is created from black and cream stripes with a diaper design in primrose. The 24 buttons are made up of cream, purple and magenta crossing to form the character-istic death's head pattern.

Such a waistcoat would have been worn by a fashionable dandy. Rudolph Ackermann defined such a gentleman in his fashion journal, *Repository of Arts*, launched in 1806: '... a dandy was a new term for a buck or a blood; with the difference, that the dandy aimed rather more at being effeminate, and instead of being a dashing, high-spirited fellow, which "bloods" generally are, that they only wished to be thought delicate and fine and pretty.'

Detail from a waistcoat dating from the first decade of the 19th century. This is made from plain cream cotton with woven horizontal stripes in satin. The restrained decoration is applied to the centre front, pockets and lapels and is of bows and tassels in silver-gilt thread, tamboured chain stitch. The edges of the waistcoat are decorated with 5 rows of similar chain stitch also in silver-gilt thread.

By working from the under-side and using a tambour frame it was possible for the embroiderer, even working in metal thread, to produce a chain stitch with greater consistency and at a much faster rate. There are 18 cloth-covered buttons similarly decorated with circles of chain stitch surrounding chain stitch stars.

Passement is the general term for braids, gimps and laces made in a variety of threads. In the 18th century silver and gold lace using passementerie techniques were frequently used to adorn clothes, the three-dimensional qualities of the end product providing the perfect trimming to glimmer in candlelight as well as ostentatiously to display wealth. Their enormous cost made them affordable only by the very rich.

A bill dating from 1770 records the kind of prices charged by lacemen:

'6 yards. Gold plaited lace @ 15/…£4.10.0.

Gold vellum & thread to work the holes & 20 Gold spangled buttons…17.6.'

In comparison, the gentleman's 'fine Blue Cloth frock and breeches, lin'd with Ratinett & gilt buttons' only came to £4.16.6. A pound in 1770 is estimated to be the equivalent of £56.60 in today's money.

Because of the innate value of the lace it was traditional for old embroideries to be systematically unpicked for their metallic thread, a practice known as 'drizzling', making surviving examples even more treasured.

This stomacher is part of a set of silver lace robings dating from the 1740s that would have been added to the chosen dress to show the wealth and social aspirations of the wearer. The stomacher was pinned over the front of the robe, silver lace cuffs were attached to the sleeves over cotton lace cuffs, and the robings decorated the edges of the robe, as indicated in Nancy Bradfield's drawing. All these additions would be pinned in place and could be removed after wear and used for another social occasion.

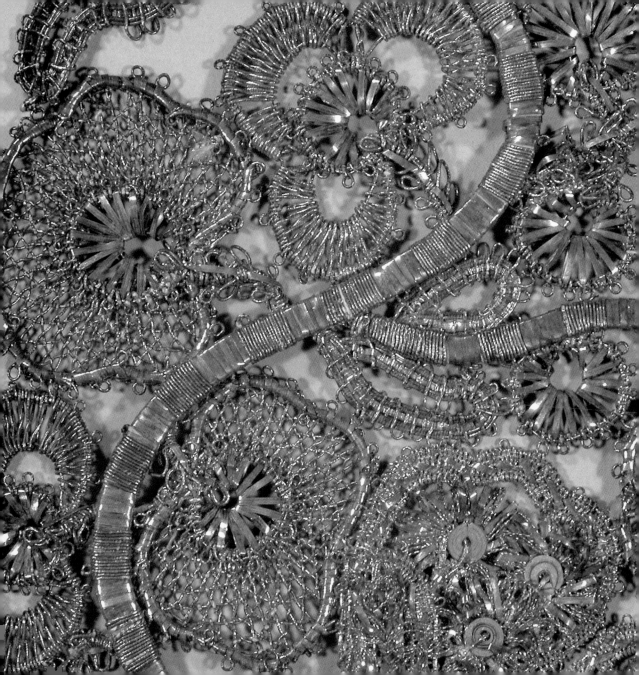

Waistcoat

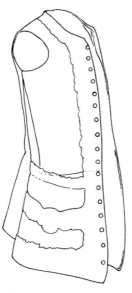

Sir Rowland Winn, 5th Baronet, with his wife, detail from a double portrait painted by Hugh Douglas Hamilton in 1767, at Nostell Priory, Yorkshire. Sir Rowland is shown wearing a waistcoat positively bristling with gold lace trimmings.

Ladies certainly did not enjoy the exclusive privilege of precious metal lace trimmings to their dresses; men's clothes and other accessories were equally likely to be adorned.

One early 18th-century advertisement regarding a theft recounts: 'Taken from a gentlemen's House – a Dove Colour'd Cloth Suit embroider'd with Silver, and a pair of Silk Stockings of the same colour; a Grey Cloth Suit with Gold Buttons and Holes; a Silk drugget Salmon Colour Suit lin'd with white silk. A Silver Brocade Waistcoat trim'd with a knotted Silver Fringe, and lin'd with white Silk.' The list goes on.

The detail shown here is from a beautiful waistcoat dating from the 1750s. It is made from deep gold silk damask decorated with an elaborate silver lace 10cms (4ins) deep on the front, hem and pocket flaps. The waistcoat is further decorated by 17 buttons of the domed shape typical of the early and mid-18th century, covered and richly embroidered with silver purl and plate.

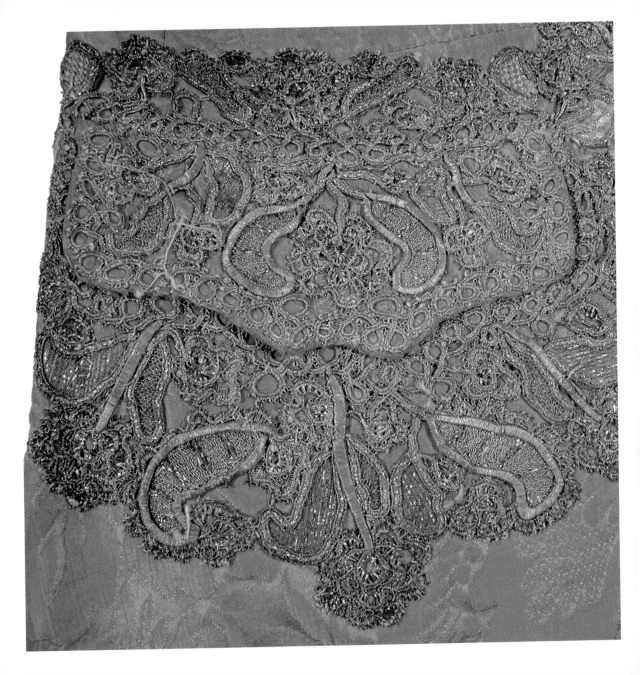

Waistcoat

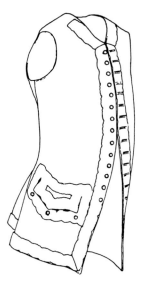

Detail from a waistcoat dating from the early 1750s, made from a delicate sky blue silk grosgrain. It is lavishly decorated with 4.5cms (1 ¾ ins) wide silver lace around the neck, the front, the hem and the pocket flaps. The basket buttons are very similar in style to those shown on pp.14-15.

Henry Purefoy of Shalstone in Buckinghamshire provides an excellent record of the way that fashion, clothing and accessories were acquired by a gentleman. His clothes were generally purchased locally or from London through tradesmen and agents who would give advice on the latest fashions and trends. In 1744

he records ordering from George Vaughan, laceman in the Strand, '5 yards of silver Lace to bind a waistcoat as good and fashionable as any is worn; and also two dozen and four silver twist buttons for the waistcoat'.

Metal lace was also used to decorate other items of costume such as the vamps of shoes. Purefoy also purchases 'enough of fashionable silver lace to lace four pairs of shoes for my mother and a yard of narrow silver lace to go up the seam behind the shoes'.

William Windham II, attributed to James Dagnia, c. 1740, now at Felbrigg Hall, Norfolk. Windham is shown in the elaborate costume of a captain of the Hungarian Hussars.

Braid is generally defined as woven or plaited cord or ribbon which is then applied, usually couched, to a garment. It has been used to trim costume in many cultures over the centuries, but the technique became significantly used in the decoration of military and civil uniforms.

In late 18th century a cross-over took place, with braiding, loops and frogging used as decoration on fashionable dress for both men and women. *The London Chronicle* for June 1778 reported how Georgiana, wife of the 5th Duke of Devonshire and very much the fashion icon of the period, gave the style a boost: 'Saturday morning the Derbyshire Militia passed through the city on their road to Cox Heath. The Duke of Devonshire marched at their head. The whole regiment made a very noble appearance, equal to any regulars whatever. If the militia of the other counties prove but as good, there is no doubt but they are a match for any force that can be brought against them. The Duchess of Devonshire followed the regiment, dressed en militaire, and was escorted by several attendants.'

These details are from a jacket of an officer in the French Hussars dating from the 1830s. It is made from a navy wool and decorated in a cotton braid. The Hussars were always known for the elaborateness of their uniform and although the braiding on this example is merely cotton, rather than the gold of dress uniform, the effect is both dramatic and stylish.

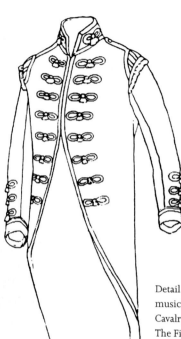

Detail from a coatee worn by a
musician in the Royal Fifeshire
Cavalry Volunteers, c. 1799.
The Fifeshire yeomanry was
originally raised as seven
independent troops in 1797
and formalised a year later. It
was disbanded in 1828.

   The coatee is made from red
napped wool, and is decorated
with chevrons of braid made
from silk-cored silver wire
and blue and white silk thread.
There are figure-of-eight loop
decorations around each button,
with fringes of pink, blue and
silk-cored silver thread. The
buttons decorating the front and
the sleeve are marked 'Firmin
& Westall, Strand', and are
decorated with a crown and 'FV'.

Thomas Legh, a portrait by William Bradley painted c. 1818, now at Lyme Park in Cheshire. Legh is shown in Middle Eastern dress, including a waistcoat rather like the example shown here and on subsequent pages.

Charles Paget Wade collected many traditional costumes from all parts of the world. In terms of craftsmanship and design, they provide interesting social and technical comparisons with the main body of his costume collection. The waistcoats and jackets from the Balkans are such a group. They mostly date from the late 19th or early 20th centuries and use braiding, sequins and metal thread to create exotic and rich patterns and designs.

The detail shown here is from a Yugoslavian waistcoat of rich purple-brown silk velvet that has been trimmed with gold lace, Russia braid and sequins. The Russia braid has been used to form a stylised and flowing floral design. The waistcoat is fastened by delicate gold filigree buttons.

Jacket

Details from a late 19th-century Greek jacket made from a light green napped wool that has been decorated with bands of padded Russia braid of silver gilt. The silver gilt is wound around a greenish gold core that gives a particular hue. There is interlaced plaited braid in loops either side of the front opening and a border of small coils on the collar. The long motif on the back of the sleeve is made up from bands of Russia braid with a smaller coiled motif at the cuff. The round buttons are covered with silver thread with a small coral bead decorating the tip of each. There are small thread-covered round buttons on the underarm seam of the sleeve and the front armhole with button loops made from a fine square cord.

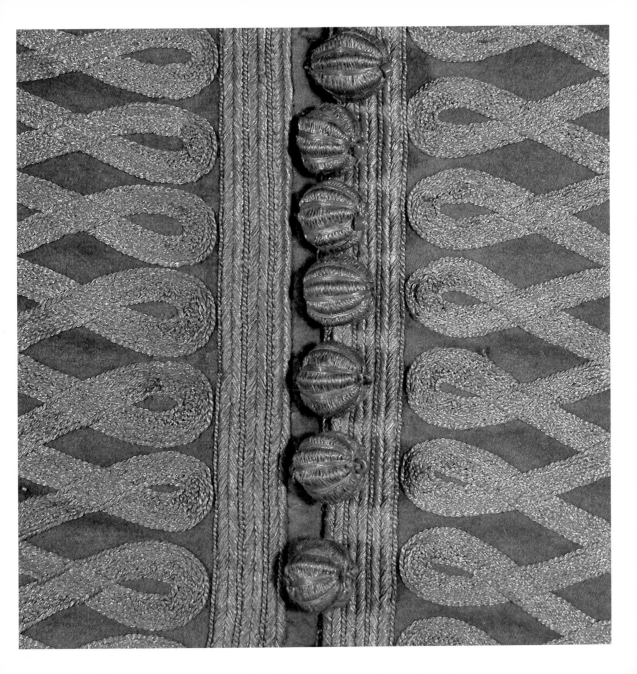

Waistcoat

Details of a waistcoat that was made in Bosnia, Herzogovina or Montenegro, *c.*1900. It is of rich ruby silk velvet decorated with two widths of narrow gold braid down the centre front and along the hem. The gold braid on the front and along the hem is couched and sewn in loops. On each side of the waistcoat is a large thistle, a leaf and a smaller flower couched in gold braid and edged with moss green Russia braid. The gold braid at the centre of the thistle is couched onto cypress green velvet.

The waistcoat closes with metallic dome-shaped buttons with engraved lines and small raised circles.

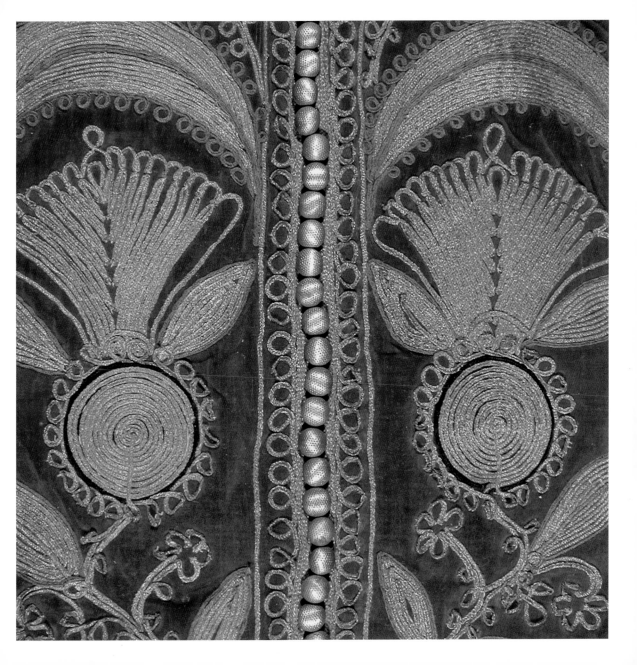

Detail from a waistcoat, again
from Bosnia, Herzogovina or
Montenegro and of a similar
date to the example shown
on pp. 40-41. This waistcoat
is made from deep plum silk
velvet. The decoration in gold
braid flows down the front of
the waistcoat in a free design
of stylised flowers and leaves.
Across each front there is one
stem of flowers and leaves.
The whole design is pulled
together by the fine metal
filigree buttons, each with
a blue glass bead at its apex.
The effect of the whole is not
dissimilar to the decorated
gentlemen's court coats of the
18th century shown earlier.

Bonnet

Traditionally the finest straw for hats and bonnet manufacture came from Leghorn, now Livorno in Tuscany. This produced a fine plait such as on this early 19th-century poke bonnet, woven in a spiral from the centre back.

The form of the poke bonnet evolved as a result of the influence of classicism on all aspects of dress. Hair was cropped and framed the face, while the poke bonnet loosely emulated an idealistic if rather inaccurate notion of the classical profile. Along with the blue and cream flowered ribbons that tied under the chin, the modest decoration of the braid around the brim fulfils the stylistic requirement of classical simplicity whilst displaying delightful attention to detail. The braid shown here is made from horsehair and straw plait.

By the 1840s, fancy braids made from a variety of materials such as straw, horsehair, cotton and string were used in the manufacture of bonnets. Supplies from the Continent were interrupted by wars in the late 18th and early 19th centuries, boosting the strawmaking industry at home. Plait schools were established in the English Midlands, Bedfordshire and Hertfordshire and here children as young as three were taught the intricacies of straw plaiting in return for a rather meagre education. The industry thrived until cheap imports from Italy and from sources further afield, such as China, made it uneconomical causing considerable poverty in these areas.

Milliners would either sell the straw hats untrimmed or trim them to order. Horsehair and straw were often used in combination for the main body of the bonnet.

This bonnet, dating from the 1840s, employs bands of horsehair, cotton and straw braids alternating with black and cream straw mesh. It is trimmed with swathed blue silk ribbons crossing at the top and a ribbon bavolet at the back of the bonnet which is also edged with a narrow straw braid. The whole is finished with a posy of flowers, leaves and buds centre front.

Stomachers

Detail from a portrait of the Hervey family painted by Hubert-François Gravelot in 1750, now at Ickworth in Suffolk. The foremost of the ladies is wearing a pink stomacher decorated with ribbon bows with her open robe and pink apron.

Pinking was a widely used technique for edging fabric to prevent fraying. Without the ease of modern pinking shears, the process of stamping the pinked edge was laborious. However, it produced a distinctive and highly decorative effect that was used to enhance many 18th-century costumes.

The two stomachers, dating from around 1750, are a good example of the versatility of the technique. They come with an open robe of the same material – a silk and wool mix of the most intense yellow. The mix of fibres gives the fabric a delicate sheen and slight crispness. Each stomacher is decorated with pleated and pinked trim of self-fabric of different designs. One has definite signs of having been pinned, the usual method for attaching.

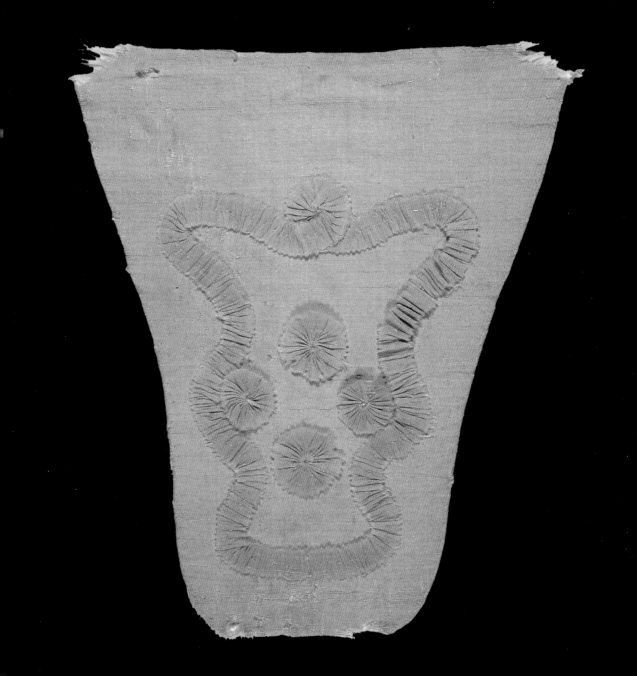

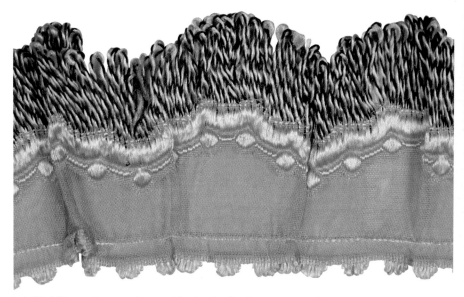

In 1685, following Louis XIV's Revocation of the Edict of Nantes, many Huguenot refugees fled from France to Britain, bringing with them their skill at weaving and setting up communities in the silk industry. One specialising in weaving ribbons was established at Spittlemore in Coventry. Initially their workshops constituted a cottage industry, but in the early 19th century the weaving became increasingly mechanised and small factories were created. The community thrived until the removal of protective duty on foreign imports of ribbon in the 1860s, causing the home industry to decline.

The details of 19th-century ribbons shown here and on the following pages demonstrate the richness of variety and design available. The market was supplied by shops and travelling salesmen such as Parson Woodforde recounts in his diary for 1781: 'One Mr Alldridge who goes about with a cart with Linen, Cottons, Laces etc called at the house this morning to know if we wanted anything in his way'.

As the 19th century progressed and more people had disposable wealth, the market flourished. The bonnet was a perfect medium for effecting change and displaying individuality through

decorative artistry. This is well illustrated by Lydia Bennett in Jane Austen's *Pride and Prejudice*: 'Look here, I have bought this bonnet. I do not think it is very pretty; but I thought I might as well buy it as not. I shall pull it to pieces as soon as I get home, and see if I can make it up any better.... I have bought some prettier-coloured satin to trim it with fresh, I think it will be very tolerable.'

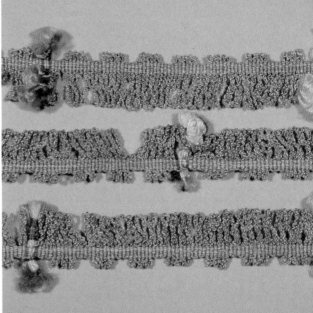

Evening Bonnet

With the end of the Napoleonic Wars in 1815, France began once more to influence fashions in dress, especially for ladies. Moving away from the classical elegance and modesty of the Regency style, the waists of dress moved down, skirts rose, sleeves ballooned into huge gigots, and bonnets became large and extravagant. This example of an evening bonnet, dating from the 1820s, is a wonderful example both of the changing fashion and the potential ribbons provided for adding style and extravagance.

The bonnet is made from ivory silk trimmed with two large wings of silk with wired edges on the crown side. The trimmings are large and made from wide Cambridge blue silk gauze ribbon. Silk gauze was one of the most desirable and expensive of available trimmings, often imported from the French town of St Etienne where at this time around 100,000 people were employed in ribbon manufacture.

Loops are held in shape with narrow blue wired ribbon and there are the same blue ribbon trimmings inside the brim. Typically the trimmings are all pinned into place.

Detail of a caricature by George Cruikshank, lampooning the fashion excesses of 1827. The figure featured here wears a tall hat covered in fancy ribbons and plumes of feathers, atop a wasp-waisted dress with huge gigot sleeves.

This bonnet dating from the early 1830s is more restrained in its decoration than the evening hat shown on pp. 54-55. However, it is of similarly generous proportions in a shape known derogatorily as chimney pot. It is made from Leghorn straw, which continued to be the finest and most desirable straw available for millinery (see pp.44-45).

By this time milliners had established themselves as a profession in most towns, supplying not just the hats trimmed and untrimmed but a range of purchasable trimmings. The simplicity of this style offered endless scope for trimming and re-trimming with ribbons, an occupation suitable for young ladies at leisure at home. In 1814, Jane Austen wrote in a letter: 'Ribbon trimmings are all the fashion at Bath … . I have been ruining myself in black satin ribbon with a proper perl edge; & now I am trying to draw it up into kind of Roses, instead of putting it in plain double plaits'.

This Leghorn bonnet is trimmed with a headband of cream ribbed silk which is decorated with small brocaded flower motifs. This is probably a later addition to the bonnet, as is the band of ruched cream chiffon and narrow green ribbon around the brim.

By the late 1830s, fashion was very much influenced by the young Queen Victoria, who ascended the throne in 1837. Emphasis shifted from size and flamboyance to demure modesty. Bonnets became close fitting, with the sides of the brim curved down over the ears to form an oval frame for the bun and side ringlets popular at this period.

This bonnet is made from a 7-end plaited straw which has been hand-stitched through the overlapped plait. Although the fashions may have become more modest, the trimmings continued to be of great importance. These are of wide striped, ribbed silk ribbon, which forms a band with a large bow that passes over the top of the crown and brim. The lower edge of the bonnet is precisely pleated and ruched and held in place by strategically placed pins.

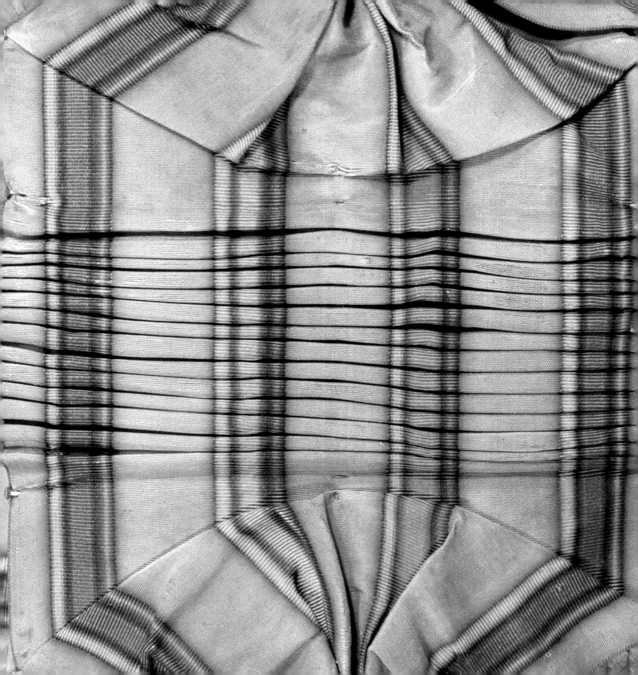

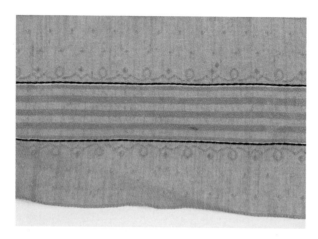

A bonnet dating from 1850, made from a narrow straw plait that has been painted and stiffened to form a very hard fabric. The matt appearance of the straw provides a perfect foil for the beautiful, wide, sapphire-blue satin ribbon which has been masterfully pleated and ruched around the lower edge of the bonnet. The ribbon extends into the fashionable long lappets. The back section of pleating is pinned and held in place with a piece of red painted card behind to provide some degree of support for the ribbon.

In strong contrast to the blue satin ribbon decoration, wide grey and green brocade ribbons (detail shown above) are pinned to the inside of the brim as fastenings.

Bonnet

Feathers provide an ideal trimming, especially for hats. They have form, tactile qualities, sheen and colour. They can be cut, shaped and dyed and in many cases can be used again and again.

This richly coloured bonnet, dating from the 1840s, is made from a burgundy ribbed fabric of wool and silk with maroon satin. The crown and sides of the bonnet are trimmed with a red feather decoration dyed to match the colour of the fabric. Wide maroon silk ribbons hang from the points of the bonnet.

As the 19th century proceeded, so the use and abuse of nature reached heights that led to demands for legislation and control. Whole birds as well as the individual feathers were often used, threatening enormous numbers of species. A single consignment of birds from South America might contain 40,000 humming birds to provide aigrettes for millinery, and in 1895 it was reckoned 'some twenty to thirty million dead birds are imported into this country annually to supply the demands of murderous millinery'. Finally the ladies of Manchester had enough of murderous millinery and in protest formed the Fur, Fin and Feather Group which became the Royal Society for the Protection of Birds.

Fanchon Bonnet

Fanchon bonnets became fashionable in the late 1860s. An innovation of the Parisian couturier Charlesworth, their name was derived from the French for 'kerchief'. *The Ladies Treasury* of 1866 described them as 'no longer bonnets, but plaques of lace trimmed with the tiniest flowers'.

This example would have been worn placed towards the front of the head over a chignon. It curves down over the ears with a frill at the back of cream machine lace, and has a band across the forehead. It is made from pastel yellow satin and silk georgette in rows of box pleats across the bonnet. It is edged with machine blonde-style lace with a satin bow centre front. The bar is decorated with cornflowers, poppies and ferns of coloured, stiffened cotton. The trim is brought to life with the striking white daisies made from feathers.

The bonnet is actually fastened by wide yellow satin ribbons that tie beneath the chignon, but it also has false ties of georgette and satin held with satin and lace bows at the throat and narrow ties of cream silk-fringed ribbon.

Artifical Flowers

Flowers are one of the most available and obvious ways of trimming costume and the art of making artificial flowers has been practised for thousands of years. Examples have been found in Egyptian tombs, and the Romans were known to wear perfumed flowers made from papyrus or silk. By the 18th century centres producing a wide variety of such trimmings were established throughout Europe, notably in Paris and Lyons. Industrialisation during the 19th century led to mass production which fed the insatiable appetite of the thriving middles classes.

The two examples shown on the right date from the 19th century. The flowers and leaves on the far right are made from starched cotton with stems of covered wire. On the near right, the flowers are made from feathers.

The detail shown above is from a stylish straw hat of the 1930s. Fastened on to the heavy black silk net is a decoration of stamped pink velvet in the form of a bunch of grapes.

Reticule

One of the more unusual trims that became popular in the 19th century was the use of fish bones and scales. Fish bones were often used for objects such as calling card cases woven in a similar manner to cane. For embroidery it was usually the scales that were used. Scales of perch, carp and goldfish were gathered, cleaned and sometimes tinted. They would then be soaked and cut and pierced ready for use in embroidered designs. Eventually this passion for novelty, which also included designs using feathers and insect wings, led to accusations of exploitation.

This reticule, dating from c.1830, has a beautiful design of leaves and flowers made from chenille, fish scales, ribbon work and silk embroidery. The base fabric is a deep purple-black satin with a pink silk lining. It is edged with black silk fringe and there are black silk ribbon handles.

Sequins, also known as paillettes, were traditionally made by coiling a circular silver wire tightly around a long core of wood or metal. The coil was cut along its length with a fine saw, releasing a series of small wire rings that were then hammered to form perfect circles with a central hole. There was a vast range of sizes available to the embroiderer who took every opportunity to exploit the potential for adding effect to the design so well illustrated in these details of the pocket flap of a court coat dating from the 1780s.

Cascades of sequins held in place with silver purl, metal thread, paste jewels and silk embroidery combine to form an exotic design of flowers and leaves. The base fabric is fancy silk velvet with a pattern of voided stripes and squares in black, pink and green. The buttons which decorate the pockets, the cuffs and the front also pick up elements of the design with sequins, paste jewels and silver thread (see also pp.6-7).

Details of the front and pocket flap from the coat of a complete suit dating from the 1770s (see also pp.10-11). It was quite unusual for the three elements of a suit to be made of the same material at this time. In 1785 *The Lounger* reported 'I desired my taylor to make me a plain suit of clothes; next day he brought me a blue frock, a scarlet waistcoat, with gold buttons, and a pair of black silk breeches. I should have preferred a plain suit all of a piece but he shut my mouth, saying it was quite the fashion, that everybody wore it.'

The base fabric is a most intricate cut and uncut velvet of purple stripes lifted by small yellow dots. The very nature of the velvet implies great expense, as the manufacture involved the introduction of pile warps into a normal set of warps and wefts. The extra pile warp is woven over metal wires which are then pulled through, cutting the warp loops and forming the tufts that create the velvet pile.

The embroidery, a flowing design of flowers and leaves carried through the three pieces of the suit, is executed in a relatively thick white silk thread. The sequins and paste jewels have been added to give the design the characteristic three-dimensional quality.

Details of a late 18th-century coat of beetroot silk velvet, showing the front edges and a pocket flap richly embroidered with silver threads and sequins of silver-plated copper in a design of palm trees and other foliage. Large flat buttons covered with silver foil also have a decoration of silver threads and paste jewels (see pp.12-13).

At this period there was much similarity between English and French fashions. Felix Hezecques wrote of Louis XVI: 'On Sundays and ceremonial occasions his suits were of very beautiful materials, embroidered in silks and paillettes. Often, as the fashion then was, the velvet coat was entirely covered with little spangles, which made it very dazzling.'

Shoulder Cape

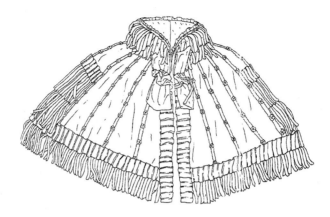

Detail from a shoulder cape dating from c. 1900, made from blue/brown shot silk giving an iridescent sheen. By this period, ladies' costumes had become extravagantly bedecked. A commentator reported in 1887 that the effect being sought was rich and glittering, with 'gauging, frills, ribbon bows, lace, metal beads, artificial pearls … trimmed with sequins, transparent dewdrops, birds and butterflies.'

This cape is trimmed with radiating lines of a complex braid made up from blue and gold sequins and beading. It is additionally adorned with frills and fripperies of all descriptions. A deep pleated frill of self-fabric decorates the outer edges, with several layers on the collar. There are three panels of double rows of frills at the sides and back. Black striped, box-pleated silk ribbon decorates the front edge and along the pleated frilling. There is a thick black satin ribbon bow either side of the front neck and one at the centre back neck with three tails, one sewn down at the end.

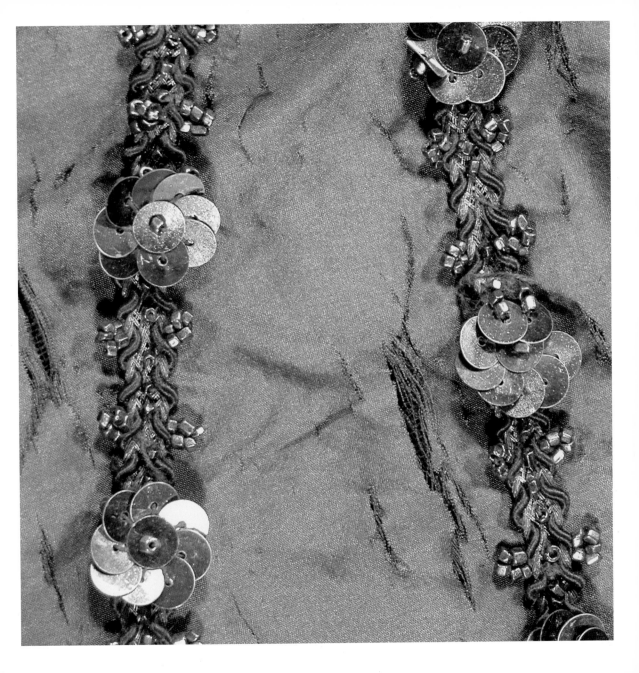

Detail from an illustration of mens' and boys' fashion from the Gazette of Fashion for January 1857.

A late 19th-century cap made from spectrum blue, ivory and black velvet. The voided brocade patterns consist of stylised flowers and leaves around the base of the cap, and on top a design of silver sequins and coiled gold purl over a padded base of cream wool. A long gold tassel of coiled wire is attached to the crown.

One of the more benign results of the Crimean War was that cigarette smoking became fashionable in Britain. However, ladies objected to the smell. Queen Victoria, for instance, insisted on Prince Albert directing the smoke from his cigars and cigarettes up the chimney. Rooms were set aside for smoking, often combined with billiards, and men were encouraged to wear special, loose-fitting jackets and matching caps, as can be seen in the fashion plate shown here. Caps usually took the form of a pill-box with a hanging tassel, and were embroidered, as with this example, in patterns that resembled Turkish costume.

Spencer

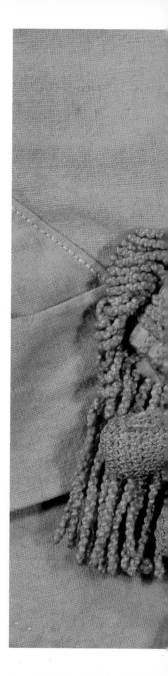

Just as the Huguenots were experts at weaving silk ribbons, they were also skilled at creating tassels of silk thread wound around a core for trimming upholstery and for very elaborate costume. Their arrival in numbers from France following the Revocation of the Edict of Nantes in 1685 provided an important boost to the development of both the upholstery and dressmaking trades.

The tassels shown here are made of silk and cord, and decorate the centre back of a yellow brown cotton spencer dating from the Regency period. The spencer was a short-waisted, long-sleeved jacket named after George John, 2nd Earl Spencer, who allegedly burned the tails of his coat whilst warming himself by the fire thus beginning a new fashion. The tailless short jacket was worn by both sexes, but most particularly by women in the early 19th century, as it provided a valuable layer of warmth over the figure-hugging, light dresses. In 1799 Parson Woodforde recorded in his diary: 'Though June, it was very cold indeed today, so that Mrs Custance came walking in her Spencer with a Bosom-friend [tippet to protect the throat and chest]'.

*Mary Ann Bullock, ex-dairy maid
and chatelaine of Uppark in Sussex, a
photograph from the mid-19th century.*

82

Details of tassels from a bodice of green and pink shot silk taffeta dating from 1850.

Colours at this time tended to be subtle and in harmony with the trim and decoration, as in this example where the tassels and braid of silk brocade enhance the richness of the shot silk. The trimming runs down the front and lower edges of the bodice, and in three scalloped rows at the lower sleeves, as in a similar costume shown in the photograph of Mary Ann Bullock.

The green and pink silk bodice is one of a pair of the same fabric but slightly different design. It would have been worn with a matching skirt to complete the outfit. Skirts were increasing in circumference, supported on cage crinolines. Advice was given to young ladies 'not to attempt the climbing of stiles in a crinoline for the task is impossible; and if she suffers much from the comments of vulgar little boys it would be better, in a high wind, to remain indoors'.

Purse

This little purse, dating from the late 17th century, is typical of the style popular throughout Europe for carrying money or for gambling tokens. Although quite worn, something of its richness is still discernible. It is made from a deep peony-red silk velvet. Velvet, being highly labour intensive and complex to manufacture, by its very nature denotes expense and richness.

The purse is decorated with a band of silver lace and a delightful tassel of twisted silver and bows.

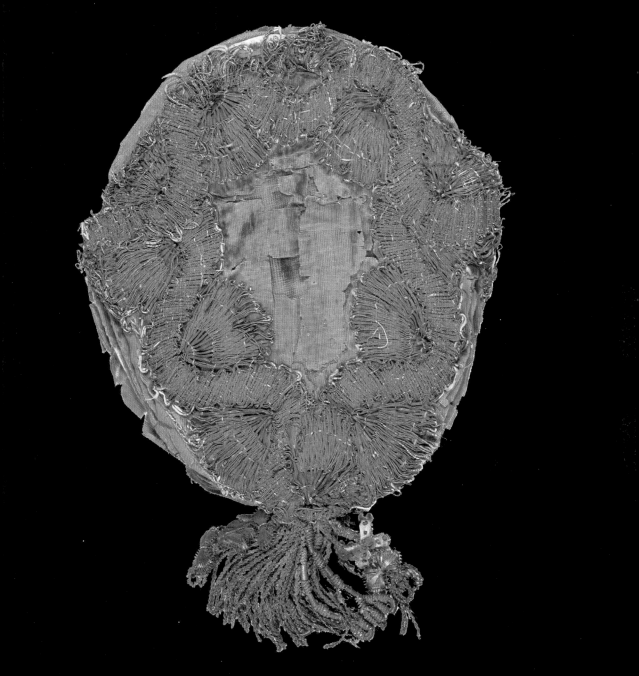

Drawstring Purse

An early 19th– century purse made from knitted silk with horizontal stripes of black and geranium pink silk and gold-coloured metal thread. On either side are painted ivory medallions in gilt surrounds with scenes, probably of the Madeleine and the Place de la Concorde in Paris. There are triple tassels of graded geranium pink and cream silk thread headed with plaited gilt wire. The same type of tassels hang from a silver cord and decorate the sides of the purse.

This example is known as a thimble or guinea purse, later called the sovereign purse after the introduction of that denomination in 1816. They were often attached to ready-made clasps or, like this example, made with a drawstring.

Such delicate purses came into increasing use during the 18th and 19th centuries, and were often made at home and given as gifts. Catherine Hutton, born in 1756, the daughter of a successful businessman from Birmingham, describes some of the activities she undertook in the home that would have been quite normal for a young woman: 'I have worked embroidery on muslin, satin and canvas and netted upwards of one hundred wallet purses'.

Reticules

Details from two silk canvas reticules dating from the 1830s. Right, a cream silk canvas bag embroidered on both sides with wool and silk. The side shown here has shades of green with a pink rosebud and gilt beads highlighting the design. The edges are bound with cream silk cord and the top with cream silk satin. Cream chenille tassels decorate either side of the opening.

Chenille, a soft velvety thread that takes its name from the French for caterpillar, had been popular as an ingredient of tassels from the 17th century. The thread is formed by weaving a material in which the warp threads are arranged in groups of two to six ends. These interlace like a gauze with the groups a definite distance apart according to the desired length of pile. The woven piece is cut into warp-wise strips which are then used as the weft yarn. The result is an intensity of colour unsurpassed by any other embroidery medium.

The detail of a chenille tassel (above) is from a very similar reticule, embroidered in three shades of blue and grey with steel spangles and gilt beads.

Reticule

A tassel, one of four in the shape of pine-cones in silver and green foil, attached with loops of silver thread to an early 19th-century reticule. The reticule itself (not shown) is of cream silk satin with a hand-painted design of flowers attached to a silver frame decorated with daisies. Such ready-made frames were sold so that reticules could be made up and embroidered at home, and thus coordinate with an outfit. They were available in all shapes and sizes, as were an endless variety of trimmings. Contemporary domestic magazines for young ladies invariably presented innovative designs and suggestions for such pursuits, feeding the growing demand from a class of young ladies keen to display their prowess through activities such as sewing and painting.

The reticule, ridicule or indispensable developed during the later years of the 18th century as a practical solution to changing fashion. Prior to their adoption as receptacles for female essentials, pockets had been suspended from the waist under the petticoat. These proved impractical when dresses in fabrics like muslin and fine cotton lawn were too light and diaphanous to disguise bulky pockets.

Bergère Hat

An 18th-century milkmaid wearing her bergère, from an engraving by Shepherd after H.W.Bunbury.

The versatility of straw as a creative medium, even for producing tassels, is displayed wonderfully on this 18th-century bergère hat. The main form of the hat is woven from split straw plait in a chequered pattern of dyed black and natural straw. A band of brown fancy straw plait decorates the brim edge and a band of macramé straw braid with split straw the brim. The hat is further trimmed around the crown with a garland of split straw cord and tassels.

The bergère was a very popular style of the 18th century. The large, flat-brimmed hat was traditionally associated with older women and servants until it was adopted by the young and the fashionable. Charles de Saussure, a visitor from Switzerland, commented in 1727: 'Ladies even of the highest rank are thus attired when they go walking or make a simple visit'. It soon became a repository for all manner of trimmings such as feathers, flowers and ribbons, growing in size to accommodate the ever-increasing desire for display. According to *The Gentleman's and London Magazine* of 1777: 'The trimmings are raised to an extravagant height, of multi-coloured ribbon, artificial flowers and one or two black or white feathers, partly upright at the back of the crown. Gaily disposed young ladies wear them turned up behind with a bow and streamers.'

Glossary

BAVOLET the back ruffle or curtain on a bonnet

BERGÈRE from the French for shepherd. A flat hat with a low crown and brim of varying width, usually made from straw

BRAID woven or plaited cord or ribbon

CHENILLE From the French for caterpillar. A tufted cord of silk or worsted with a pile that makes it resemble a hairy caterpillar

FANCHON a small decorative bonnet that became fashionable in the 1860s. The crown and brim merged with the brim, curving over the ears to form a low oval around the face. Fanchons provided an ideal medium for trimmings of all sorts

FOIL a thin leaf of metal used in embroidery and as a backing for paste jewels

GIGOT from the French for fiddle. Also known as leg of mutton and applied to the shape of sleeves in the early 19th century

GROSGRAIN from the French gross grain – coarse texture. A ribbed silk

LEGHORN fine straw imported from Livorno, Tuscany, Italy

PAILLETTES silver sequins

PASSEMENTERIE fancy edging or trimming made from braid, beading, metallic thread

PASTE a brilliant glass of high lead content used for making imitation gems

PLATE a flat piece of metal used in metal thread embroidery

PURL a thread of twisted gold or silver wire used for embroidery or edging

RUSSIA BRAID a flat woven braid

First published in Great Britain in 2004
by National Trust Enterprises Limited,
36 Queen Anne's Gate
London SW1H 9AS

www.nationaltrust.org.uk

ISBN 0 7078 0387 X

Designed by SMITH

Editorial and picture research by Margaret Willes
Colour origination by Digital Imaging Ltd. Glasgow
Printed in China by WKT Co.Ltd.

Picture Credits
The Wade Collection pictures were photographed by Richard
Blakey. Other illustrations: NTPL/Derrick E.Witty, pp.6, 92;
NTPL/Andreas von Einsiedel, pp 8, 10;
NTPL/John Hammond, pp.14, 20, 28, 32, 36, 54, 78;
NTPL/Angelo Hornak, p.48; NT, p.82.

Cover: Early 19th-century drawstring purse (see pp.86 and 87)
Half-title: Tassel from a 19th-century reticule (see pp.90 and 91)
Frontispiece: Detail of a sleeve from a jacket of the Fifeshire
    Yeomanry (see pp. 34 and 35)
Title: Late 19th-century smoking cap (see pp. 78 and 79)